Grammar
Practice Book

Grade 3

SCHOOL PUBLISHERS

www.harcourtschool.com

ISBN 10   0-15-349910-9
ISBN 13   978-0-15-349910-4

            20   0868   15   14   13
4500426660

If you have received these materials as examination copies free of charge, Harcourt School
Publishers retains title to the materials and they may not be resold. Resale of examination
copies is strictly prohibited and is illegal.

Possession of this publication in print format does not entitle users to convert this
publication, or any portion of it, into electronic format.

Contents

Contents

Grammar Practice Book
© Harcourt • Grade 3

Name _____

▶ **Rewrite each group of words to form a statement that makes sense. Use capital letters and end marks correctly.**

1. Vaughn on Maple Street lives

   _____

2. he a student new is

   _____

3. math he enjoys

   _____

4. flute the he plays

   _____

5. from London is Andrea

   _____

6. science she good is at

   _____

7. lives she near park the

   _____

8. she likes dance to

   _____

9. teaches Mr. Jackson third grade

   _____

10. He the welcomes children new

   _____

Grammar Practice Book
© Harcourt • Grade 3

▶ **Rewrite each group of words to form a question
that makes sense. Use capital letters and end
marks correctly.**

1. you do a brother have

   _____

2. what his name is

   _____

3. he to school go does

   _____

4. he read can

   _____

5. play he does where

   _____

▶ **Turn each statement into a question. Use the word
in parentheses ( ) as the first word.**

6. My little sister's name is Sara. (What)

   _____

7. She copies everything I do. (Why)

   _____

8. She meets me after school. (When)

   _____

9. She wants to go to the store. (Where)

   _____

Name _____

▶ **Read this part of a student's rough draft. Then answer the questions that follow.**

(1) I to like skip. (2) Why do I skip (3) it is more fun than walking. (4) I skip all the way to school (5) With my friends at recess. (6) _____ you like to skip, too?

1. In which sentence are the words in an order that does NOT make sense?
   A Sentence 1
   B Sentence 2
   C Sentence 4
   D Sentence 5

2. Which sentence does not tell a complete thought?
   A Sentence 1
   B Sentence 3
   C Sentence 4
   D Sentence 5

3. Which sentence should end with a question mark?
   A Sentence 2
   B Sentence 3
   C Sentence 4
   D Sentence 5

4. Which sentence is missing a period?
   A Sentence 1
   B Sentence 2
   C Sentence 4
   D Sentence 5

5. Which word in Sentence 3 should be capitalized?
   A is
   B it
   C way
   D fun

6. Which word would make sense in the blank in Sentence 6?
   A Why
   B But
   C Do
   D Where

3

Name _____

▶ **Add the correct end mark to each sentence.
Then label each as a *statement* or a *question*.**

1. Where is the teacher _____   _____

2. I do not like to jump _____   _____

3. When does Anita run _____   _____

4. Do you know Mr. Wang _____   _____

5. We play in the grass _____   _____

▶ **Rewrite each group of words to form a statement or a
question. Put the words in an order that makes sense.
Use capital letters and end marks correctly.**

6. to the park I go (statement)

   _____

7. do walk you to school (question)

   _____

8. Willow ball the throws (statement)

   _____

9. can Kurt play softball (statement)

   _____

10. you can football play (question)

   _____

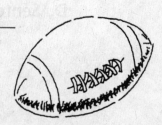

4

▶ Rewrite each sentence, using capital letters and
end marks correctly. Then label each as a *command*
or an *exclamation.*

1. give the book to Violet

    _____

2. what a great author he is

    _____

3. how excited I am to read his new story

    _____

4. let your brother read

    _____

5. oops, I lost the book

    _____

6. help me find it

    _____

7. search in the living room

    _____

8. wow, it is a mess in here

    _____

9. hurray, here it is

    _____

10. look at the pretty cover

    _____

Grammar Practice Book
© Harcourt • Grade 3

▶ **Rewrite each sentence, using capital letters and
end marks correctly. Then label each as a *statement*,
a *question*, a *command*, or an *exclamation*.**

1. Cathy wants to be a writer

   _____

2. read Cathy's story

   _____

3. what does she write about

   _____

4. what a good writer Cathy is

   _____

▶ **Add words and end marks to make four kinds of sentences out of the
words in the box.**

the	things	Cathy	does

5. a question

   _____

6. a statement

   _____

7. an exclamation

   _____

8. a command

   _____

▶ **Read this part of a student's rough draft. Then answer the questions that follow.**

(1) Wow, today was an exciting day. (2) What an interesting time we had (3) A firefighter visited our school. (4) Our teacher how to prepare. (5) She told us to think of questions to ask the firefighter (6) What question do you think I asked.

1. Which sentence should end with an exclamation point?
 A Sentence 1
 B Sentence 4
 C Sentence 5
 D Sentence 6

2. Which sentence should end with a question mark?
 A Sentence 1
 B Sentence 3
 C Sentence 4
 D Sentence 6

3. Which end mark should Sentence 2 have?
 A a period
 B a comma
 C a question mark
 D an exclamation point

4. Which end mark should Sentence 5 have?
 A a period
 B a comma
 C a question mark
 D an exclamation point

5. Which sentence is not complete?
 A Sentence 1
 B Sentence 3
 C Sentence 4
 D Sentence 6

6. Which sentence is correct?
 A Sentence 2
 B Sentence 3
 C Sentence 4
 D Sentence 6

▶ **If the sentence is complete, add a correct end mark. If the sentence is not complete, write *not a sentence*.**

1. My father is an author _____

2. How he loves to write _____

3. How do I help him _____

4. Things that he can write about _____

5. Read his latest book _____

6. Wow, it's exciting _____

▶ **Add words and end marks to make four kinds of sentences. Each sentence is started for you.**

7. a statement

You _____

8. a command

Go _____

9. an exclamation

What _____

10. a question

What _____

Grammar Practice Book
© Harcourt • Grade 3

Name _____

▶ **Underline the simple subject. Write the predicate.**

1. Lisa went to boarding school.

   _____

2. My good friend learned at home.

   _____

3. He rode the bus to school.

   _____

4. His older sister studied dance.

   _____

5. I went to school.

   _____

6. Leroy enjoyed college.

   _____

7. The high school student worked on Sundays.

   _____

8. Dad helped my brother.

   _____

9. The little girl painted pictures.

   _____

Try This

Choose four sentences from a book or magazine. Write the sentences.
Underline the simple subjects.

Name _____

▶ **Underline the complete predicate. Write the simple predicate.**

1. Hannah likes math.

   _____

2. Science is my favorite subject.

   _____

3. Jamil studies French every day.

   _____

4. My cousin wears a uniform to school.

   _____

5. The teacher plans her lesson carefully.

   _____

6. The boys clean their desks.

   _____

7. The children read quietly.

   _____

8. Some students use a computer.

   _____

9. Everyone enjoys the class trip.

   _____

10. Valerie practices the trumpet.

   _____

Grammar Practice Book
© Harcourt • Grade 3

▶ **Read this part of a student's rough draft. Then answer the questions that follow.**

> (1) My little brother is five years old. (2) He goes to kindergarten. (3) Kindergarten fun. (4) The young children learn with toys and games.

1. Which is the complete subject of Sentence 1?
   A My little
   B brother
   C My little brother
   D is five years old

2. Which is the complete predicate of Sentence 1?
   A is
   B five years old
   C My little brother
   D is five years old

3. Which is the simple subject of Sentence 2?
   A He goes
   B to kindergarten
   C He
   D goes

4. Which is the simple predicate of Sentence 2?
   A He
   B goes
   C goes to kindergarten
   D to kindergarten

5. Which is the complete subject of Sentence 4?
   A The young children
   B children
   C children learn
   D learn

6. Which sentence does NOT have a correct predicate?
   A Sentence 1
   B Sentence 2
   C Sentence 3
   D Sentence 4

Name _____

▶ **Add a complete subject to each predicate.**
Then underline the simple subject.

1. _____ went to school.

2. _____ played outside.

3. _____ ate lunch.

4. _____ took a nap.

5. _____ performed on stage.

6. _____ was made of brick.

▶ **Add a complete predicate to each subject. Then underline the simple**
predicate.

7. An art teacher _____.

8. The excited children _____.

9. He _____.

10. My mother _____.

11. The school _____.

12. The tired baby _____.

12

▶ **Rewrite each pair of sentences as one sentence.
Draw one line under each compound subject and
two lines under each compound predicate.**

1. Juan played the piano. His sister played the piano.

   _____

2. The children worked hard. The children practiced every day.

   _____

3. Music filled the room. Laughter filled the room.

   _____

4. Michelle wanted to write poems. Diego wanted to write poems.

   _____

5. They wrote in their notebooks. They studied with a teacher.

   _____

6. My uncle went to school. My uncle learned to cook.

   _____

7. Carmen loved soccer. Her cousin loved soccer.

   _____

8. They played together. They won trophies.

   _____

9. Mr. Han's students talked. Mr. Han's students made plans.

   _____

▶ **Write the compound subject of each sentence.
Add commas where they belong.**

1. Ravi his grandmother and his grandfather went to the school concert.

_____

2. Ravi's teacher his neighbor and his friend were in the audience.

_____

3. The violins cellos and flutes sounded beautiful.

_____

4. The drums cymbals and gong played an exciting ending.

_____

5. A tall woman a short man and a child left the hall first.

_____

▶ **Write the compound predicate of each sentence. Add commas where
they belong.**

6. Ravi went home changed into pajamas and climbed into bed.

_____

7. He lay down fell asleep and dreamed he was a musician.

_____

8. He played a solo bowed and smiled at the audience.

_____

9. The audience stood up clapped and cheered.

_____

▶ **Read this part of a student's rough draft.
Then answer the questions that follow.**

> (1) Madeline and Ella were sisters. (2) They wanted to be doctors when they grew up. (3) Their mother shared their goal. (4) Their father shared their goal. (5) The girls worked hard and got good grades. (6) They got into a special school succeeded and became doctors.

1. Which sentence has a compound subject?
   A Sentence 1
   B Sentence 2
   C Sentence 5
   D Sentence 6

2. Which sentence needs commas to separate the compound predicates?
   A Sentence 1
   B Sentence 2
   C Sentence 5
   D Sentence 6

3. Which sentences could be joined to make one sentence with a compound subject?
   A Sentences 2 and 3
   B Sentences 3 and 4
   C Sentences 4 and 5
   D Sentences 5 and 6

4. Which sentence has a compound predicate that is written correctly?
   A Sentence 1
   B Sentence 3
   C Sentence 5
   D Sentence 6

5. Which of these sentences does NOT have a compound subject or a compound predicate?
   A Sentence 1
   B Sentence 2
   C Sentence 5
   D Sentence 6

6. Which of these possible final sentences has a compound subject?
   A Their dream came true.
   B The sisters and their parents had a dream that came true.
   C They healed and cured.
   D People admired them.

▶ **Add a compound subject or a compound
predicate to complete each sentence.**

1. _____ studied art.

2. The athletes _____.

3. The music student _____.

4. _____ took dance classes.

5. The actor _____.

6. _____ watched the stars.

▶ **Rewrite each sentence. Add commas where they belong.
Draw one line under each compound subject and two lines
under each compound predicate.**

7. The soccer player ran kicked and scored.

_____

8. Exercise rest and healthful food made the swimmer strong.

_____

_____

9. Raja his sister and his brother were good students.

_____

_____

10. The scientist wrote a book won a prize and gave a speech.

_____

_____

▶ **Read this part of a student's rough draft.
Then answer the questions that follow.**

(1) There is something new in Room 112 (2) Can you guess what it is (3) our rabbit has four babies. (4) How tiny the bunnies are! (5) Wish could take one home. (6) Do you bunnies like?

1. Which sentence should end
   with a period?
   A Sentence 1
   B Sentence 2
   C Sentence 4
   D Sentence 6

2. Which sentence should end
   with a question mark?
   A Sentence 1
   B Sentence 2
   C Sentence 3
   D Sentence 4

3. In which sentence are the
   words in an order that does not
   make sense?
   A Sentence 2
   B Sentence 3
   C Sentence 4
   D Sentence 6

4. Which word in Sentence 3
   should be capitalized?
   A our
   B rabbit
   C four
   D babies

5. Which of the following is NOT
   a complete sentence?
   A Sentence 1
   B Sentence 3
   C Sentence 4
   D Sentence 5

6. Which sentence is correct as
   it is?
   A Sentence 3
   B Sentence 4
   C Sentence 5
   D Sentence 6

► **Read this part of a student's rough draft.
Then answer the questions that follow.**

(1) Eric watched the news on TV. (2) His father watched the news on TV. (3) The newscaster talked about special events. (4) A police officer a firefighter and a teacher taught third graders about safety. (5) The mayor took a trip and gave a speech.

1. Which is the simple subject of Sentence 1?
   A Eric
   B Eric watched
   C the news
   D watched the news on TV

2. Which is the complete predicate of Sentence 3?
   A the newscaster
   B the newscaster talked
   C talked
   D talked about special events

3. What is missing in Sentence 4?
   A commas
   B a subject
   C a simple predicate
   D a complete predicate

4. Which sentence has a compound subject?
   A Sentence 1
   B Sentence 3
   C Sentence 4
   D Sentence 5

5. Which sentence has a compound predicate?
   A Sentence 2
   B Sentence 3
   C Sentence 4
   D Sentence 5

6. Which sentences could be joined to make one sentence with a compound subject?
   A Sentences 1 and 2
   B Sentences 2 and 3
   C Sentences 3 and 4
   D Sentences 4 and 5

▶ **If the sentence is complete, label it as *simple* or
compound. If it is a fragment, add words to make
it complete.**

1. My big sister has a job.

   _____

2. After school.

   _____

3. She works at a pet store.

   _____

4. She feeds the animals, and she cleans their cages.

   _____

5. Sweeps the floor.

   _____

6. My sister enjoys her job, but she also likes weekends.

   _____

7. She spends time with friends, or she relaxes at home.

   _____

8. My brother is sixteen, and he works on weekends.

   _____

9. He packs bags at a supermarket.

   _____

10. My family.

   _____

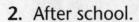

Grammar Practice Book
© Harcourt • Grade 3

Name _____

▶ **Use the words in the parentheses ( ) to join the pairs of sentences. Use commas correctly.**

1. Today is Sunday. Andy goes to a football game. (and)

   _____

2. He is excited. He eats breakfast quickly. (and)

   _____

3. Linda wants to go with Andy. She is sick. (but)

   _____

4. Andy's mother goes to the game. His father stays home. (but)

   _____

5. Tanya has strong legs. She loves to run. (and)

   _____

6. She likes softball. She likes basketball more. (but)

   _____

7. Some children play in the gym. Anna plays in the park. (but)

   _____

8. It is a hot day. Children sell lemonade. (and)

   _____

9. Darnell likes lemonade. He likes milk more. (but)

   _____

10. He walks to the store. He buys milk. (and)

   _____

Grammar Practice Book
© Harcourt • Grade 3

▶ **Read this part of a student's rough draft. Then answer the questions that follow.**

(1) Maya is a third grader, or she helps her family. (2) She washes the dishes, and she waters the plants. (3) Also cleans her room. (4) Maya's father makes breakfast most mornings. (5) Today he leaves early for work. (6) Maya's brother cooks eggs, he serves them to his family.

1. Which sentence is NOT complete?
   A Sentence 2
   B Sentence 3
   C Sentence 4
   D Sentence 5

2. Which sentence is a correct compound sentence?
   A Sentence 1
   B Sentence 2
   C Sentence 4
   D Sentence 6

3. Which sentence has an incorrect joining word?
   A Sentence 1
   B Sentence 2
   C Sentence 5
   D Sentence 6

4. Sentence 5 is _____.
   A missing a joining word
   B not complete
   C a simple sentence
   D a compound sentence

5. Which word would BEST follow the comma in Sentence 6?
   A and
   B but
   C or
   D today

6. Which sentences could be joined with a comma followed by *but*?
   A Sentences 1 and 2
   B Sentences 3 and 4
   C Sentences 4 and 5
   D Sentences 5 and 6

▶ **Rewrite the sentences. Use commas and joining words correctly.**

1. My father is a teacher and he works at a school.

_____

2. He drives to work, he takes a bus.

_____

3. He has lunch at work or he eats in the park.

_____

4. Most days he eats tuna, today he eats egg salad.

_____

▶ **Rewrite each pair of sentences as one sentence. Use commas and the joining words *and* or *but* correctly.**

5. Mrs. Lopez loves to read. She owns a bookstore.

_____

6. The store is small. It has many books.

_____

7. Sasha works with animals. She enjoys her job.

_____

8. She lives in the country. She works in the city.

_____

Grammar Practice Book
© Harcourt • Grade 3

Underline the common nouns. Circle the proper nouns.

1. Officer Chan is from Dallas, Texas.

2. Marta has a dog named Rufus.

3. The family adopts two tiny kittens.

4. Fish swim in the Atlantic Ocean.

5. Kangaroos and koalas live in Australia.

6. Steve visits the big zoo in Los Angeles.

7. The children see a pretty deer.

8. There are many seals in Canada and Greenland.

9. Charlie rides a black horse at the fair.

10. Mr. Jones feeds the birds in Central Park.

11. People watch bats in Gainesville, Florida.

12. Buffy is a white dog, and Puff is an orange cat.

Try This

Find an article in a magazine. List five common nouns from the article. Then list five proper nouns.

Grammar Practice Book
© Harcourt • Grade 3

▶ **Rewrite each sentence correctly. Capitalize the proper nouns.**

1. A zookeeper came to class on thursday.

   _____

2. Emma got a rabbit on valentine's day.

   _____

3. On saturday we visited the animal park.

   _____

4. The children learned about the first thanksgiving.

   _____

5. The first day of winter was wednesday, december 21.

   _____

6. Presidents' day was in february.

   _____

7. Which holiday was on friday, november 11?

   _____

8. Elijah went to the beach every sunday in july.

   _____

9. The family went on vacation in december.

   _____

10. The memorial day picnic was on monday, may 28.

    _____

▶ **Read this part of a student's rough draft. Then answer the questions that follow.**

(1) Robin and Pam are sisters, and they live in Michigan. (2) Their family got a new puppy on labor day. (3) Daisy is a guide dog, and she will help blind people when she grows up. (4) The children and their parents raise the puppy. (5) Every _____ they go to a dog training class in Detroit.

1. Which word in Sentence 1 is a common noun?
   A Robin
   B sisters
   C live
   D Michigan

2. Which word or words in Sentence 2 should be capitalized?
   A family
   B new
   C puppy
   D labor day

3. Which of these words in Sentence 3 is NOT a noun?
   A Daisy
   B dog
   C grows
   D people

4. How many nouns are in Sentence 4?
   A 1
   B 2
   C 3
   D 4

5. A proper noun belongs in the blank in Sentence 5. Which word is correct?
   A Saturday
   B week
   C Holiday
   D april

6. Which sentence does NOT have a proper noun?
   A Sentence 1
   B Sentence 3
   C Sentence 4
   D Sentence 5

Grammar Practice Book
© Harcourt • Grade 3

▶ **Rewrite each sentence correctly.**

1. danny has a Partner in the classroom.

    _____

2. Her Name is ann.

    _____

3. Danny and ann study every Afternoon.

    _____

4. On fridays the Children learn math.

    _____

▶ **Rewrite each sentence correctly. Underline the**
common nouns. Circle the proper nouns.

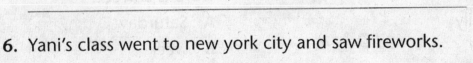

5. Independence day was on tuesday.

    _____

6. Yani's class went to new york city and saw fireworks.

    _____

7. Lights filled the sky over the hudson river.

    _____

8. The Students wrote a report about their trip.

    _____

Name _____

▶ **Write the abbreviations for the underlined words.**

1. Jean-Luc visits the <u>United States</u>.

   _____

2. Springfield is a city in <u>Illinois</u>.

   _____

3. <u>Doctor</u> Witky lives on Pine <u>Road</u>.

   _____

4. Tanisha is from <u>New Mexico</u>, but now she lives in <u>Washington</u>.

   _____

5. The police station is on the corner of East <u>Street</u> and North <u>Avenue</u>.

   _____

6. <u>Oregon</u> is next to <u>California</u>.

   _____

7. <u>Mistress</u> Rosen owns a house in <u>Rhode Island</u>.

   _____

8. Write to <u>Mister</u> Ngo at 122 Long <u>Avenue</u>, Gary, <u>Indiana</u>.

   _____

9. Lake Erie is north of <u>Ohio</u>, <u>Pennsylvania</u>, and <u>New York</u>.

   _____

10. <u>Doctor</u> Harrison takes a bus from <u>Mississippi</u> to <u>Alabama</u>.

   _____

▶ **Write the abbreviation for each word.**

1. January

   _____

2. Saturday

   _____

3. Wednesday

   _____

4. March

   _____

5. September

   _____

6. Friday

   _____

▶ **Correct the abbreviations.**

7. Oct 19

   _____

8. aug. 25

   _____

9. mon, feb. 5

   _____

10. tues, nov 9

    _____

Grammar Practice Book
© Harcourt • Grade 3

► **Read this part of a student's rough draft. Then answer the questions that follow.**

(1) _____ Block studies the animals in the ocean.
(2) He came to our school on <u>Thursday</u>, December 29.
(3) Our school is in ME. (4) He drove his car from MA.
(5) The students in <u>Mistress</u> Lewis's class enjoyed his talk.

1. Which abbreviation could go in the blank in Sentence 1?
   A Mr
   B mr
   C Mr.
   D dr.

2. Which is the correct abbreviation for the underlined word in Sentence 2?
   A thu.
   B TH
   C Thurs
   D Thurs.

3. Which is the correct abbreviation for the month in Sentence 2?
   A Dec.
   B dec.
   C DE
   D dec

4. Which word should replace the abbreviation in Sentence 3?
   A Massachusetts
   B Maine
   C Minnesota
   D Mississippi

5. Which word should replace the abbreviation in Sentence 4?
   A Massachusetts
   B Maine
   C Minnesota
   D Montana

6. Which is the correct abbreviation for the underlined word in Sentence 5?
   A Mrs
   B Mrs.
   C Ms
   D Ms.

▶ **Write the full word for each abbreviation.**

1. FL _____

2. Tues. _____

3. Dr. _____

4. St. _____

5. Apr. _____

▶ **Find the words in each sentence that have abbreviations. Write the abbreviations.**

6. Mister Ward's party is on Sunday, November 5.

_____

7. Send the letter to Doctor Johnson at 5 Mesa Street, El Paso, Texas.

_____

8. In September, Mistress Torres's class goes to the animal shelter on River Avenue.

_____

9. Tennessee and Missouri are next to Kentucky.

_____

10. Mistress Brecht spoke at the school on Barstow Road on Friday.

_____

Rewrite each sentence using the plural form of the underlined noun. Use the word in parentheses ( ) before each plural noun.

1. Ari bakes a <u>cake</u>. (two)

   _____

2. He puts them in a <u>box</u>. (two)

   _____

3. Please buy a <u>banana</u>. (some)

   _____

4. We need a <u>bunch</u>. (three)

   _____

5. Lily picks a <u>berry</u>. (ten)

   _____

6. Marco wants a <u>cookie</u>. (four)

   _____

7. Abby eats a <u>pear</u>. (two)

   _____

8. She gives her sister a <u>cherry</u>. (five)

   _____

9. My father cuts a <u>pepper</u>. (two)

   _____

10. My brother eats a <u>bite</u>. (three)

    _____

Grammar Practice Book
© Harcourt • Grade 3

Name _____

▶ Rewrite each sentence using the plural form of
the underlined noun. Use a dictionary if you
need to. Each new sentence is started for you.

1. One child had cereal for breakfast.

   Three _____

2. One woman baked brownies.

   Two _____

3. One mouse ran to the food bowl.

   Three _____

4. One deer pulled leaves from the tree.

   Four _____

5. One goose ate the bread.

   Five _____

▶ Rewrite each sentence. Replace the singular nouns in
parentheses ( ) with the plural form. Use a dictionary
if you need to.

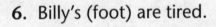

6. Billy's (foot) are tired.

   _____

7. Billy and the (man) cook soup for dinner.

   _____

8. After dinner he brushes his (tooth).

   _____

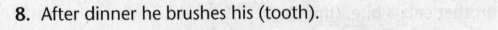

Grammar Practice Book
© Harcourt · Grade 3

Name _____

▶ **Read this part of a student's rough draft. Then answer the questions that follow.**

> (1) It is Josh's turn to set the table. (2) He uses his family's best <u>dish</u>. (3) He takes out a <u>fork</u> and spoons. (4) He puts out glasses for the men and women. (5) He puts out cups for the <u>child</u>. (6) Now _____ can be served.

1. Which is the correct plural form of the underlined word in Sentence 2?
   A dishs
   B dishies
   C dishes
   D dish

2. Which is the correct plural form of the underlined word in Sentence 3?
   A forkes
   B forks
   C forkies
   D fork

3. Which word in Sentence 4 is NOT a plural noun?
   A puts
   B glasses
   C men
   D women

4. The underlined word in Sentence 5 should be in its plural form. Which is correct?
   A child
   B childs
   C childes
   D children

5. A singular noun belongs in the blank in Sentence 6. Which word is correct?
   A dinners
   B dineries
   C dinner's
   D dinner

6. Which sentence does NOT have a plural noun?
   A Sentence 1
   B Sentence 3
   C Sentence 4
   D Sentence 5

Name  _____

▶ **Write the correct plural form of each singular noun. Use a dictionary if you need to.**

1. pot _____

2. raspberry _____

3. tomato _____

4. meal _____

5. rabbit _____

6. moose _____

7. sheep _____

8. puppy _____

▶ **Rewrite the sentences. Use the plural forms of the nouns in parentheses ( ). Use a dictionary if you need to.**

9. The (child) made (sandwich).

_____

10. Amber sliced (carrot) and (apple).

_____

11. Do you want (blueberry) or (peach)?

_____

12. Brush your (tooth) after you eat the (strawberry).

_____

Grammar Practice Book

© Harcourt • Grade 3

► **Read this part of a student's rough draft. Then answer the questions that follow.**

> (1) Mrs. Sanchez's class performed a play on _____, October 2. (2) The Play was at the Madison Elementary School. (3) At 7:00 P.M. (4) My sister Elaine acted, she did a great job. (5) My bedtime is 8:00 P.M. (6) My parents let me stay up late to watch the play.

1. Which word could go in the blank in Sentence 1?
   A Monday
   B tuesday
   C evening
   D lunchtime

2. Which word in Sentence 2 is incorrectly capitalized?
   A Play
   B Madison
   C Elementary
   D School

3. Which word should follow the comma in Sentence 4?
   A but
   B or
   C and
   D tonight

4. Which is the proper noun in Sentence 4?
   A sister
   B Elaine
   C great
   D job

5. Which two simple sentences could be joined by a comma followed by *but*?
   A Sentences 1 and 2
   B Sentences 3 and 4
   C Sentences 4 and 5
   D Sentences 5 and 6

6. Which sentence is NOT complete?
   A Sentence 2
   B Sentence 3
   C Sentence 5
   D Sentence 6

▶ **Read this part of a student's rough draft.
Then answer the questions that follow.**

> (1) There is a mystery to solve at 10 Mountain <u>Road</u>.
> (2) The Brooks children can't find their puppy. (3) What
> are the clue? (4) The door is open, and cookies are baking
> in the house across the street. (5) _____ Brooks says she
> knows where the puppy is. (6) Do you?

1. What is the abbreviation for
   the underlined word in
   Sentence 1?
   A rd
   B rd.
   C Rd.
   D RD

2. What is the correct plural form
   of the noun in Sentence 3?
   A clue
   B clues
   C cluees
   D cluies

3. How many SINGULAR nouns
   are in Sentence 4?
   A two
   B three
   C four
   D five

4. How many PLURAL nouns are
   in Sentence 4?
   A one
   B two
   C three
   D four

5. Which abbreviation could go
   in the blank in Sentence 5?
   A mrs
   B Mrs
   C MS
   D Mrs.

6. Which sentence has an
   irregular plural noun?
   A Sentence 2
   B Sentence 3
   C Sentence 4
   D Sentence 5

Name _____

▶ **Write the possessive noun in each sentence.**
  Label it as *singular* or *plural*.

1. Rico's family has three children.

   _____

2. My brothers' toys are on the floor.

   _____

3. Her sister's name is Kristen.

   _____

4. Mason rides in his aunt's car.

   _____

5. The families' homes are nearby.

   _____

6. The boys' grandfather comes to visit.

   _____

7. What is your mother's job?

   _____

8. Shane wears his cousin's hat.

   _____

9. Mr. Daly enjoys his sons' softball game.

   _____

10. The dog's leash is on the table.

   _____

37

▶ **If the underlined word needs an apostrophe ('), rewrite it correctly. If it is correct, write *correct*.**

1. Ms. Roth held her <u>daughters</u> hand. _____

2. The <u>schools</u> auditorium was full. _____

3. The <u>boys</u> performed in a play. _____

4. My <u>fathers</u> camera was broken. _____

5. The student read two <u>poems</u>. _____

6. How many <u>songs</u> did they sing? _____

▶ **Write the plural form of each noun. Then write the plural possessive form.**

7. uncle _____

_____

8. grandson _____

_____

9. violinist _____

_____

10. glass _____

_____

11. cherry _____

_____

12. banana _____

_____

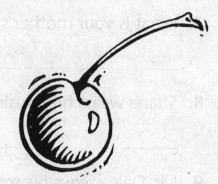

Grammar Practice Book
© Harcourt • Grade 3

▶ **Read this part of a student's rough draft.
Then answer the questions that follow.**

> (1) Mr. Kwon class put on a show. (2) The students families were in the audience. (3) The student's performed different acts. (4) The act of Rachel was funny. (5) Rachel's parents smiled and clapped. (6) All the parents enjoyed the show.

1. Which singular possessive noun should be a plural noun?
   A show (Sentence 1)
   B audience (Sentence 2)
   C student's (Sentence 3)
   D act (Sentence 4)

2. Which singular noun should also be possessive?
   A Mr. Kwon (Sentence 1)
   B audience (Sentence 2)
   C act (Sentence 4)
   D show (Sentence 6)

3. Which plural noun should also be possessive?
   A students (Sentence 2)
   B families (Sentence 2)
   C acts (Sentence 3)
   D parents (Sentence 5)

4. How could you rewrite the underlined phrase in Sentence 4?
   A the act's of Rachel
   B the acts of Rachel
   C Rachel's act
   D Rachels' act

5. Which other word could replace *parents* in Sentence 6?
   A parents'
   B families'
   C students'
   D families

6. Which sentence is correct as it is written?
   A Sentence 1
   B Sentence 2
   C Sentence 3
   D Sentence 5

Name _____

► **Rewrite each phrase. Use the correct possessive noun.**

1. the costumes that belong to the girls

   _____

2. the dance of Ron

   _____

3. the necklace owned by her grandmother

   _____

4. the bottles of the babies

   _____

5. the sleeves of the dresses

   _____

6. the car that belongs to my mother

   _____

► **Write sentences using the noun below. The words in parentheses ( ) tell which form of the noun to use.**

dancer

7. (singular) _____

8. (plural) _____

9. (singular possessive) _____

10. (plural possessive) _____

40

▶ **Write the two singular pronouns in each sentence.**

1. She sent me a postcard.

   _____

2. Where did he put it?

   _____

3. I gave her the box.

   _____

4. It was a gift for you.

   _____

5. You spoke to him today.

   _____

6. He saw you yesterday.

   _____

7. She told me the story.

   _____

8. I enjoyed reading it.

   _____

9. You wrote a letter to her.

   _____

10. Did it interest him?

    _____

41

Name _____

▶ **Write the plural pronoun in each sentence.**

1. We took a flight to Mexico. _____

2. My aunt and uncle met us at the airport. _____

3. They smiled and said "Welcome!" _____

4. My sister was excited to see them. _____

▶ **Rewrite each sentence. Use a plural pronoun to replace each underlined phrase.**

5. The <u>girls</u> went to camp last summer.

_____

6. The girls wrote to <u>my friend and me</u>.

_____

7. <u>My friend and I</u> wrote to the girls.

_____

8. My friend and I told <u>the girls</u> about our soccer team.

_____

9. Did <u>you and your brother</u> send letters to the girls?

_____

10. The girls were happy to get <u>the letters</u>.

_____

11. <u>The letters</u> arrived every Monday.

_____

12. They just got a letter from <u>Mom and Dad</u>.

_____

▶ **Read this part of a student's rough draft.
Then answer the questions that follow.**

> (1) Natasha has a pen pal named Chen. (2) Chen lives in China. (3) Natasha and Chen write every week. (4) Natasha and Chen tell each other about the things they do. (5) Last week Natasha wrote to Chen about the school play. (6) Natasha told him that everyone enjoyed the play.

1. Which sentence has a singular pronoun?
   A Sentence 1
   B Sentence 3
   C Sentence 4
   D Sentence 6

2. Which sentence has a plural pronoun?
   A Sentence 1
   B Sentence 3
   C Sentence 4
   D Sentence 6

3. Which pronoun could replace the underlined word in Sentence 2?
   A He
   B Him
   C They
   D It

4. Which pronoun could replace the underlined words in Sentence 4?
   A He
   B She
   C They
   D Them

5. Which pronoun could replace the underlined word in Sentence 6?
   A It
   B She
   C Her
   D They

6. Which word(s) could be replaced by the pronoun *it*?
   A Natasha (Sentence 1)
   B Natasha and Chen (Sentence 3)
   C week (Sentence 5)
   D the play (Sentence 6)

▶ **Write the pronoun in each sentence.**
Then label each as *S* (singular) or *P* (plural).

1. We learned about Chile today. _____

2. Mr. Edwards showed us two maps. _____

3. He hung the maps on the wall. _____

4. They showed volcanoes and a desert. _____

5. The students looked at them carefully. _____

6. Mr. Edwards asked me to point to the desert. _____

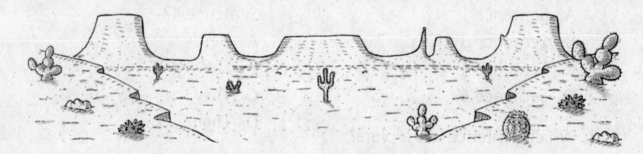

▶ **Rewrite each sentence with a correct pronoun.**

7. Ellen studied Spanish because _____ wanted to visit Spain.

_____

8. The class was fun, and the students enjoyed _____.

_____

9. The teacher brought pictures to show _____.

_____

10. He took the pictures when _____ was in Spain.

_____

Grammar Practice Book
© Harcourt • Grade 3

Name _____

▶ **Write the pronoun in each sentence. Then
label each pronoun as *subject* or *object*.**

1. Ms. Edison teaches us about flowers.

   _____

2. A student asks her how flowers grow.

   _____

3. Ms. Edison answers him.

   _____

4. She talks to the class about sunlight.

   _____

5. Flowers need it to make food and grow.

   _____

6. We learn more about flowers.

   _____

7. Bees collect pollen from them.

   _____

8. I write a paper on flowers.

   _____

[**Try This**]
Find four sentences in a book or magazine that have pronouns.
Copy the sentences. Underline the subject pronouns. Circle the object
pronouns.

Grammar Practice Book
© Harcourt • Grade 3

▶ **Rewrite each sentence. Use subject pronouns correctly.**

1. Me and Anna went to the library.

   _____

2. I and she studied trees.

   _____

3. You and me looked at books and pictures.

   _____

4. Me and he learned about pine trees.

   _____

5. I and Deon wrote a report together.

   _____

▶ **Rewrite each sentence. Use object pronouns correctly.**

6. Show the flowers to Ryan and I.

   _____

7. My mother gave me and my sister a plant.

   _____

8. Please help him and I with the report.

   _____

9. Jenny came to the library with him and I.

   _____

10. The librarian offered to help me and Ryan.

   _____

Grammar Practice Book
© Harcourt • Grade 3

Name _____

▶ **Read this part of a student's rough draft. Then answer the questions that follow.**

(1) <u>Me and my mother</u> planted an apple seed in a pot. (2) We watered the seed. (3) <u>The seed</u> grew leaves and roots. (4) My mother moved it to the yard. (5) I watched <u>my mother</u> pack soil around the little plant. (6) One day the seed will become an apple tree.

1. Which sentence has a singular subject pronoun?
   A Sentence 2
   B Sentence 3
   C Sentence 4
   D Sentence 5

2. Which sentence has a plural subject pronoun?
   A Sentence 2
   B Sentence 4
   C Sentence 5
   D Sentence 6

3. Which type of pronoun is *it* in Sentence 4?
   A singular subject pronoun
   B plural subject pronoun
   C singular object pronoun
   D plural object pronoun

4. How should the underlined phrase in Sentence 1 be written?
   A My mother and me
   B Me and her
   C Her and me
   D My mother and I

5. Which of these could replace the underlined words in Sentence 3?
   A a singular subject pronoun
   B a plural subject pronoun
   C a singular object pronoun
   D a plural object pronoun

6. Which of these could replace the underlined words in Sentence 5?
   A a singular subject pronoun
   B a plural subject pronoun
   C a singular object pronoun
   D a plural object pronoun

▶ **Write a subject or object pronoun to replace
each underlined word or phrase.**

1. Ariel's sister taught <u>Ariel</u> about bees. _____

2. <u>Ariel's sister</u> told Ariel that bees are insects. _____

3. <u>Ariel and I</u> watched bees in the park. _____

4. Ariel and I saw <u>the bees</u> fly. _____

5. Ariel's father gave <u>Ariel and me</u> a book. _____

6. <u>The book</u> had pictures of bees. _____

▶ **Rewrite each sentence. Use *I* and *me* correctly.**

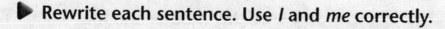

7. You and me picked pears from the tree.

_____

8. Todd ate cherries with my friend and I.

_____

9. Me and my brother sliced apples.

_____

10. They shared the plums with me and him.

_____

▶ **Write the correct pronoun for each sentence.
Then write the noun that it refers to.**

1. A bird catches worms and brings (it/them) back to the nest.

   _____

2. A mouse eats the crumbs that (it/they) finds.

   _____

3. The dogs see the man, and (him/they) start to bark.

   _____

4. John sees Michael and waves to (him/them).

   _____

5. Squirrels gather nuts and hide (it/them).

   _____

6. A spider spins a web and traps flies in (it/them).

   _____

7. Bats eat the insects that (it/they) catch.

   _____

8. Simon sees two little kittens and stops to pet (him/them).

   _____

9. A bear goes into a cave, where (it/they) sleeps all winter.

   _____

10. The boys buy a gift for Mrs. Johnson and give it to (her/them).

   _____

Grammar Practice Book
© Harcourt • Grade 3

Name _____

▶ **Rewrite each sentence. Replace the underlined word or phrase with a pronoun.**

1. Luis hugs Beth and welcomes <u>Beth</u> home.

   _____

2. Beth smiles at Luis and thanks <u>Luis</u>.

   _____

3. <u>My sister</u> invites Beth to play in the garden.

   _____

4. Luis goes to the garden too, and <u>Luis</u> plants flowers.

   _____

5. Beth finds an anthill when <u>Beth</u> is in the yard.

   _____

6. John makes dinner while <u>John</u> is in the kitchen.

   _____

7. He bakes cookies for Janet and gives them to <u>Janet</u>.

   _____

8. Janet eats a cookie, and <u>Janet</u> thanks John.

   _____

9. John is pleased because <u>John</u> loves to bake.

   _____

10. Janet buys John a cookbook and gives <u>the cookbook</u> to him.

   _____

▶ **Read this part of a student's rough draft.
Then answer the questions that follow.**

> (1) Mr. Kay lives in a house that <u>Mr. Kay</u> built. (2) The house is high up in the hills, and it is far from the city. (3) Mr. Kay likes the hills because <u>the hills</u> have a great view of the city. (4) Mr. Kay's children drive up a winding road when she come to visit. (5) <u>The children</u> love their father and enjoy visiting _____.

1. Which pronoun could replace the underlined words in Sentence 1?
   A he
   B she
   C they
   D it

2. Which pronoun could replace the underlined words in Sentence 3?
   A he
   B she
   C they
   D it

3. Which pronoun could go in the blank in Sentence 5?
   A it
   B them
   C him
   D her

4. Which word does the pronoun *it* refer to in Sentence 2?
   A house
   B high
   C hills
   D city

5. Which sentence has a pronoun that does not agree with the noun it refers to?
   A Sentence 1
   B Sentence 2
   C Sentence 3
   D Sentence 4

6. Which pronoun could replace the underlined words in Sentence 5?
   A It
   B Them
   C They
   D He

▶ **Circle the pronoun in each sentence. Rewrite the sentence. Correct the pronoun so that it agrees with the underlined word.**

1. The <u>nest</u> was too high for Maria to see him.

   _____

2. <u>Maria</u> was excited because he saw an owl.

   _____

3. <u>Luke</u> was homesick when it went to camp.

   _____

4. The <u>girls</u> invited Hillary to play with her.

   _____

5. John wrote a <u>letter</u> and sent them home.

   _____

6. <u>John's</u> parents wrote back to it.

   _____

▶ **Fill in each blank with a correct pronoun. Then underline the word or words that the pronoun refers to.**

7. Honeybees live in hives, where _____ have jobs to do.

8. Worker bees feed the queen bee and protect _____.

9. Honeybees gather nectar and use _____ to make honey.

10. Some people keep bees and collect honey from _____.

Grammar Practice Book
© Harcourt • Grade 3

▶ **Read this part of a student's rough draft.
Then answer the questions that follow.**

> (1) Tony is the friend of Joan. (2) Tony tells Joan that he is upset. (3) Joan asks he what is wrong. (4) Tony says that he lost his mothers pen. (5) Joan helps him look for the pen. (6) Together they find it under Tony's bed.

1. Which sentence has a singular possessive noun?
   A Sentence 2
   B Sentence 3
   C Sentence 5
   D Sentence 6

2. Which sentence has an incorrectly written possessive noun?
   A Sentence 2
   B Sentence 3
   C Sentence 4
   D Sentence 6

3. Which phrase could replace the underlined phrase in Sentence 1?
   A the friend's of Joan
   B the friends of Joan
   C Joan's friend
   D Joans' friend

4. Which pronoun could replace the underlined word in Sentence 2?
   A he
   B she
   C him
   D her

5. Which pronoun could replace the underlined phrase in Sentence 5?
   A it
   B her
   C him
   D them

6. Which sentence has an incorrect pronoun?
   A Sentence 3
   B Sentence 4
   C Sentence 5
   D Sentence 6

▶ **Read this part of a student's rough draft.**
Then answer the questions that follow.

> (1) Yasmin writes for a newspaper that she started. (2) She reports on what is new in school. (3) Yesterday Yasmin wrote about something that happened to her. (4) She found a kitten in the school playground. (5) Yasmin took the kitten home and gave them to her father. (6) <u>Her father</u> was happy to have the kitten.

1. Which word does the pronoun in Sentence 1 refer to?
   A Yasmin
   B writes
   C newspaper
   D she

2. Which sentence has a singular subject pronoun?
   A Sentence 2
   B Sentence 3
   C Sentence 5
   D Sentence 6

3. Which sentence has a singular object pronoun?
   A Sentence 2
   B Sentence 3
   C Sentence 4
   D Sentence 6

4. Which sentence has a pronoun that does not agree with the noun that it refers to?
   A Sentence 1
   B Sentence 2
   C Sentence 3
   D Sentence 5

5. Which could replace the underlined words in Sentence 6?
   A a singular subject pronoun
   B a plural subject pronoun
   C a singular object pronoun
   D a plural object pronoun

6. Which pronoun could replace the words *the kitten* in Sentence 5?
   A she
   B it
   C they
   D them

Name _____

▶ **Write the adjective. Then write the noun that it describes.**

1. A brown bear sat in the cave. _____

2. The bear was hungry. _____

3. The forest was big. _____

4. The raccoon saw the purple berries. _____

5. The happy raccoon ate the berries. _____

6. A small child climbed a rock. _____

7. The rock was huge. _____

8. A plant grew in a tiny pot. _____

9. The plant was green. _____

10. The pot was round. _____

11. The wolf ran through the dark woods. _____

12. The wolf was gray. _____

🪐 **Try This**

Write two sentences that could begin a story. Use at least one adjective in each sentence. Circle each adjective, and draw an arrow to the noun it describes.

Grammar Practice Book
© Harcourt • Grade 3

Name _____

▶ **Write the adjective that tells how many.**

1. Some wolves live in the forest. _____

2. Seven wolves run in the pack. _____

3. The wolf has five toes on each paw. _____

4. A wolf's coat has two layers. _____

5. Wolves howl for several reasons. _____

6. The mother wolf has six babies. _____

▶ **Write the adjective that tells how many. Rewrite the sentence. Replace the number word with an adjective that tells how many without giving an exact number.**

7. Four students wrote a story together.

_____

8. The story was about six squirrels.

_____

9. A woman read eleven stories to her children.

_____

10. There were seven pictures in the book.

_____

11. The book had ninety pages.

_____

12. Three women waited for the bus to arrive.

_____

Name _____

▶ **Read this part of a student's rough draft.
Then answer the questions that follow.**

> (1) I climbed a little tree in my friend's yard. (2) I picked cherries from the tree. (3) I gave _____ cherries to my father. (4) My father had green apples at home. (5) He made a beautiful salad with the red cherries and two green apples.

1. Which sentence has an adjective that tells how many?
   A Sentence 1
   B Sentence 2
   C Sentence 4
   D Sentence 5

2. Which sentence has an adjective that tells what color?
   A Sentence 1
   B Sentence 2
   C Sentence 3
   D Sentence 4

3. Which sentence has an adjective that tells what size?
   A Sentence 1
   B Sentence 2
   C Sentence 4
   D Sentence 5

4. Which sentence does NOT have an adjective?
   A Sentence 1
   B Sentence 2
   C Sentence 4
   D Sentence 5

5. Which is the BEST word to complete Sentence 3?
   A thin
   B some
   C unkind
   D big

6. Which sentence has the most adjectives?
   A Sentence 1
   B Sentence 2
   C Sentence 4
   D Sentence 5

▶ **Underline the two adjectives in each sentence. Then write whether each adjective tells *what kind* or *how many*.**

1. Many wolves eat five pounds of food a day.

   _____

2. A few wolves have blue eyes.

   _____

3. The coats of some wolves are white.

   _____

4. Big wolves weigh more than ninety pounds.

   _____

▶ **Rewrite the sentences. Add an adjective before each underlined noun. Use an adjective that answers the question in parentheses ( ).**

5. The apple fell from the tree. (What color?)

   _____

6. There were apples on the tree. (How many?)

   _____

7. Fatima ate the apple. (What size?)

   _____

8. I cut the apple into slices. (What shape?)

   _____

Name _____

▶ **Rewrite each sentence. Use the correct form of
the adjective in parentheses ( ).**

1. The lion is (large) than the fox.

   _____

2. The peacock has the (pretty) feathers of all the birds.

   _____

3. The bear is the (strong) animal in the forest.

   _____

4. The beetle is (tiny) than the worm.

   _____

5. The horse runs (fast) than the donkey.

   _____

6. That dog has the (loud) bark in town.

   _____

7. Sabrina's rabbit is (fluffy) than my rabbit.

   _____

8. The dolphin is the (smart) of all the ocean animals.

   _____

9. The cat is (friendly) today than it was yesterday.

   _____

10. We have the (cute) pet on the block.

    _____

▶ **Rewrite each sentence. Use *more* or *the most* correctly before each adjective.**

1. These berries are _____ delicious than those berries.

   _____

2. The cherry tree is _____ beautiful of the three trees.

   _____

3. This hike is _____ difficult than the last hike.

   _____

4. A hurricane is _____ frightening than a rainstorm.

   _____

5. Thunder makes _____ terrifying sound of all.

   _____

6. This is _____ wonderful sunrise that I have ever seen.

   _____

7. The hawk is _____ powerful bird in the forest.

   _____

8. This lake has _____ unusual fish in the state.

   _____

9. This forest is _____ enormous than the Black Hills National Forest.

   _____

10. This story is _____ interesting one I have ever read.

    _____

Grammar Practice Book
© Harcourt • Grade 3

▶ **Read this part of a student's rough draft.
Then answer the questions that follow.**

> (1) My brother is older than I am. (2) He took me camping in a big forest last weekend. (3) The forest was the beautiful place that I have ever visited. (4) The trees were tall than my house. (5) In the morning we saw a brown bear. (6) I was scared than my brother, and my scream was _____ than his!

1. Which sentence has the correct form of an adjective that compares?
   A Sentence 1
   B Sentence 2
   C Sentence 3
   D Sentence 4

2. Which adjective needs the ending -er?
   A beautiful (Sentence 3)
   B tall (Sentence 4)
   C brown (Sentence 5)
   D scared (Sentence 6)

3. Which adjective needs the word *more* before it?
   A older (Sentence 1)
   B big (Sentence 2)
   C beautiful (Sentence 3)
   D scared (Sentence 6)

4. Which adjective needs the word *most* before it?
   A older (Sentence 1)
   B beautiful (Sentence 3)
   C brown (Sentence 5)
   D scared (Sentence 6)

5. Which are the correct adjectives that compare for the adjective *big* in Sentence 2?
   A bigger, biggest
   B big, biggest
   C more big, most big
   D more bigger, most biggest

6. Which is the BEST way to complete Sentence 6?
   A more loud
   B most loud
   C louder
   D loudest

Name _____

▶ **Write the form of each adjective that compares two things. Then write the form that compares three or more things.**

1. playful _____

2. funny _____

3. afraid _____

4. important _____

5. high _____

6. exciting _____

▶ **Rewrite each sentence correctly.**

7. The raccoon was small than the fox.

_____

8. Today's sunset was lovely than yesterday's sunset.

_____

9. That cliff was the most steep one I have ever climbed.

_____

10. The river was more deeper than the stream.

_____

Name _____

► **Write the article in each sentence and the noun it introduces.**

1. Angela went to the city. _____

2. She visited a friend. _____

3. Angela's friend lived in an apartment. _____

4. They took the bus. _____

5. They went to a museum. _____

6. They saw a painting. _____

7. It had a frame. _____

8. Children played in the grass. _____

9. A bird ate pieces of bread. _____

10. The man played his violin. _____

11. The friends went home. _____

12. They took a train. _____

Try This

Find four sentences that use articles in a book or a magazine. Copy the sentences. Circle the articles. Draw an arrow from each article to the noun it introduces.

Grammar Practice Book
© Harcourt • Grade 3

▶ **Rewrite each sentence. Use *a* or *an* to fill in the blank.**

1. Jessie's older sister is _____ artist.

   _____

2. She is making _____ clay sculpture.

   _____

3. Jeff buys paper and _____ box of paints.

   _____

4. He draws some squares and _____ oval.

   _____

▶ **Rewrite each sentence. Use *a, an,* or *the* to fill in the blank.**

5. Several paintings hang on _____ white walls.

   _____

6. Abe is _____ excellent painter.

   _____

7. This is _____ biggest museum.

   _____

8. You need some paper and _____ pencil for drawing.

   _____

9. _____ young artists will have an art show.

   _____

▶ **Read this part of a student's rough draft.
Then answer the questions that follow.**

> (1) My aunt lives in _____ house in the country. I visited her last weekend. (2) On Saturday we saw a owl. (3) _____ owl was in a tree. (4) On Sunday we rode a tractor and picked apples. (5) My aunt made baked apples that night. (6) _____ apples were delicious.

1. Which of these sentences has an article that is used correctly?

   A Sentence 2

   B Sentence 4

   C Sentence 5

   D Sentence 6

2. In which sentence should the article *a* be changed to *an*?

   A Sentence 2

   B Sentence 3

   C Sentence 4

   D Sentence 6

3. Which word should fill in the blank in Sentence 6?

   A A

   B An

   C The

   D One

4. Which word would BEST fill in the blank in Sentence 1?

   A a

   B an

   C the

   D several

5. Which word would BEST fill in the blank in Sentence 3?

   A A

   B An

   C The

   D Some

6. Which sentence does NOT have an article?

   A Sentence 1

   B Sentence 3

   C Sentence 4

   D Sentence 5

Name _____

► Use the articles *a*, *an*, and *the* to write two
singular forms of each plural noun.

Examples: birds: a bird, the bird

icy roads: an icy road, the icy road

1. skyscrapers _____

2. elevators _____

3. rooftops _____

4. noisy trains _____

5. escalators _____

6. shops _____

7. airports _____

8. excited boys _____

9. red cars _____

► Write a sentence for each article. Circle the article, and underline
the noun that it introduces.

10. a _____

11. an _____

12. the _____

66

Name _____

▶ **Write the complete predicate of each sentence.
Underline the action verb.**

1. The woman walks to the market.

_____

2. She buys fruit and vegetables.

_____

3. The animals gather in the yard.

_____

4. The cows moo at the ducks.

_____

5. The sun shines brightly.

_____

6. The weather reporter predicts rain.

_____

7. The boy helps his sister.

_____

8. The children eat a good meal.

_____

9. I enjoy the folktale.

_____

10. We discuss the characters.

_____

Name _____

▶ **Underline the correct action verb in each sentence.**

1. The chicken (lay/lays) five eggs.

2. Ava (watch/watches) the little chicks.

3. I (plant/plants) corn and tomatoes.

4. He (plow/plows) the field.

5. Children (play/plays) near the barn.

6. We (sell/sells) milk and cheese.

7. The dog (bark/barks) loudly.

▶ **Choose an action verb from the box to complete
each sentence. Then write the sentence.**

| takes | carry | wakes | scratch | scatters |

8. The chickens _____ in the dirt.

_____

9. The rooster _____ everyone.

_____

10. We _____ a basket of eggs.

_____

11. Tyrell _____ eggs to the market.

_____

12. She _____ feed around the yard.

_____

Grammar Practice Book
© Harcourt • Grade 3

▶ **Read this part of a student's rough draft.
Then answer the questions that follow.**

> (1) Rosa lives in Mexico City. (2) She _____ soccer. (3) She and her father watch games together on TV. (4) One Sunday they rides a bus to a game at a stadium. (5) The home team wins. (6) The excited fans stand and cheer.

1. Which is the verb in Sentence 1?

  A Rosa

  B lives

  C in

  D Mexico

2. Which of these action verbs does not agree with its subject?

  A watch (Sentence 3)

  B rides (Sentence 4)

  C wins (Sentence 5)

  D stand (Sentence 6)

3. Which sentence has a singular subject and a verb that agrees?

  A Sentence 2

  B Sentence 3

  C Sentence 5

  D Sentence 6

4. Which action verb could complete Sentence 2?

  A like

  B enjoy

  C loves

  D play

5. Which sentence has two action verbs?

  A Sentence 3

  B Sentence 4

  C Sentence 5

  D Sentence 6

6. Which sentence has a plural subject and a verb that agrees?

  A Sentence 1

  B Sentence 3

  C Sentence 4

  D Sentence 5

Name _____

▶ **Rewrite each sentence. Use the correct form of the verb in parentheses ( ).**

1. An egg (hatch/hatches) in the nest.

   _____

2. The ducklings (follow/follows) their mother.

   _____

3. The farmer (hurry/hurries) home.

   _____

4. Mice (scurry/scurries) around the barn.

   _____

5. We (milk/milks) the cows every morning.

   _____

6. She (drive/drives) the big tractor.

   _____

7. Jessica (help/helps) my brother dry dishes.

   _____

8. They (clean/cleans) the kitchen.

   _____

Grammar Practice Book
© Harcourt • Grade 3

▶ Read this part of a student's rough draft.
Then answer the questions that follow.

> (1) There was an art show at the library yesterday. (2) Children displayed their art. (3) I showed two paintings. (4) They were the largest ones in the room. (5) There were also _____ photographs and a black sculpture. (6) The sculpture was interesting than the photographs.

1. Which sentence uses the correct form of an adjective that compares?
   A Sentence 3
   B Sentence 4
   C Sentence 5
   D Sentence 6

2. Which adjective needs the word *more* before it?
   A two (Sentence 3)
   B largest (Sentence 4)
   C black (Sentence 5)
   D interesting (Sentence 6)

3. Which adjective could be written before *Children* in Sentence 2?
   A Many
   B One
   C Hundred
   D Each

4. Which adjective that tells *what kind* could fill in the blank in Sentence 5?
   A biggest
   B tiniest
   C small
   D some

5. Which sentence has an adjective that tells *what color*?
   A Sentence 1
   B Sentence 3
   C Sentence 4
   D Sentence 5

6. Which of these sentences does NOT have an adjective?
   A Sentence 2
   B Sentence 3
   C Sentence 4
   D Sentence 5

▶ **Read this part of a student's rough draft.**
Then answer the questions that follow.

> (1) Luke interviews his mother for a newsletter at school. (2) He asks his mother questions and writes down a answers. (3) _____ questions are about his mother's job. (4) Luke's mother is a engineer. (5) She plans bridges, and people builds them. (6) Students enjoy the report that Luke writes.

1. In which sentence should the article be changed to *an*?
   A Sentence 1
   B Sentence 2
   C Sentence 4
   D Sentence 6

2. Which word could fill in the blank in Sentence 3?
   A A
   B An
   C The
   D Writes

3. Which sentence has a plural noun with an article that does NOT agree?
   A Sentence 1
   B Sentence 2
   C Sentence 4
   D Sentence 6

4. Which of these action verbs does NOT agree with its subject?
   A interviews (Sentence 1)
   B writes (Sentence 2)
   C plans (Sentence 5)
   D builds (Sentence 5)

5. Which sentence has only one action verb?
   A Sentence 1
   B Sentence 2
   C Sentence 5
   D Sentence 6

6. Which sentence has a plural subject and an action verb that agrees?
   A Sentence 1
   B Sentence 2
   C Sentence 4
   D Sentence 6

Grammar Practice Book
© Harcourt • Grade 3

▶ **Write the form of the verb *be* in each sentence.**

1. Laura is cold without her hat. _____

2. The winter was long. _____

3. The gloves are on the chair. _____

4. I am warmer now. _____

5. The girls were at home. _____

6. Julio is with Laura. _____

7. The children are at the skating rink. _____

8. Those boys were good skaters. _____

9. The lake is frozen this morning. _____

10. The grass is covered with snow. _____

11. I am tired at the end of the day. _____

12. A huge snowball is next to the house. _____

13. It is the beginning of a snowman. _____

14. We were excited to begin. _____

15. I am freezing outside. _____

Try This

Write four sentences about your classroom, using the verb *be*. Use a singular subject in two sentences and a plural subject in the other two. Underline the forms of the verb *be*.

Grammar Practice Book
© Harcourt • Grade 3

▶ **Rewrite each sentence. Choose the correct form of the verb *be* in parentheses ( ).**

1. It (is, are) summer.

_____

2. I (is, am) at the ocean.

_____

3. We (was, were) warm in the sun.

_____

4. He (is, am) in the water.

_____

5. They (was, were) with their friends.

_____

6. You (is, are) on a beach blanket.

_____

7. I (was, are) at the snack bar.

_____

8. It (is, are) next to a playground.

_____

9. They (is, are) on the swings.

_____

10. She (is, are) sleepy at the end of the day.

Grammar Practice Book
© Harcourt • Grade 3

▶ **Read this part of a student's rough draft. Then answer the questions that follow.**

> (1) My friends and I are at a park. (2) We is very happy.
> (3) Flowers are everywhere. (4) A squirrel _____ in a tree.
> (5) I smile at it. (6) Spring are my favorite season.

1. Which sentence has a form of the verb *be* that does NOT agree with the subject?
   A Sentence 1
   B Sentence 2
   C Sentence 3
   D Sentence 5

2. Which does NOT have a form of the verb *be*?
   A Sentence 1
   B Sentence 3
   C Sentence 5
   D Sentence 6

3. Which could go in the blank in Sentence 4?
   A am
   B is
   C are
   D were

4. How should the form of the verb *be* in Sentence 6 be written?
   A am
   B are
   C were
   D is

5. Which has a form of the verb *be* that links the subject to words that tell *what*?
   A Sentence 1
   B Sentence 3
   C Sentence 5
   D Sentence 6

6. Which has a form of the verb *be* that links the subject to words that tell *where*?
   A Sentence 1
   B Sentence 2
   C Sentence 5
   D Sentence 6

Name _____

▶ **Circle the form of the verb *be* in each sentence. Then write whether each links the subject to words that tell *what* or *where*.**

1. Some seals are white. _____

2. The penguin chick was fuzzy. _____

3. You were on the shore. _____

4. That shark is near a whale. _____

5. I am with my parents. _____

6. They are scientists. _____

▶ **Rewrite each sentence, using a correct form of the verb *be*. Then write *S* above each singular subject and *P* above each plural subject.**

7. Those fish _____ small and silver.

_____

8. We _____ close to the beaver's dam.

_____

9. He _____ in a wooden boat.

_____

10. The river _____ full of life.

_____

Grammar Practice Book
© Harcourt • Grade 3

Name _____

▶ **Circle the helping verb and underline the main
verb in each sentence.**

1. Some butterflies can fly long distances.

2. Moths are attracted to the light.

3. The mosquito could bite you!

4. We have seen many insects this summer.

5. She will study bees at the library.

6. I am writing a report on ladybugs.

7. The bats were looking for food.

8. You should watch that hummingbird.

9. The ducks had flown south for the winter.

10. An eagle is gliding through the sky.

11. The hawk has spotted a mouse.

12. A parrot may live for 80 years.

🪐 **Try This**

Write four sentences about your day at school, using main and helping
verbs. Circle the helping verbs. Underline the main verbs.

▶ **Circle the helping verbs, and underline the main verbs.**

1. I did not watch the sunset.

2. We will now change into pajamas.

3. I could not see the moon.

4. It was hidden behind a cloud.

5. They would not go to bed.

6. The baby has never slept through the night.

7. The dogs were already sleeping.

8. Stars are shining in the sky.

▶ **Rewrite each sentence, using a helping verb from the box.**

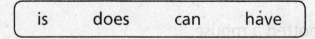

| is | does | can | have |

9. Moths _____ fly up to 25 miles per hour.

_____

10. That moth _____ not have spots on its wings.

_____

11. The butterfly _____ walking on a leaf.

_____

12. Those butterflies _____ gone to Mexico for the winter.

_____

► **Read this part of a student's rough draft. Then answer the questions that follow.**

> (1) In her dreams, Mandy can fly. (2) She gliding over the city at night. (3) The sun have set. (4) It will soon become dark. (5) Mandy loves her dream. (6) She will forget it.

1. Which has a helping verb that does NOT agree with the subject?
   A Sentence 1
   B Sentence 2
   C Sentence 3
   D Sentence 4

2. Which has a main verb and a helping verb used correctly?
   A Sentence 1
   B Sentence 2
   C Sentence 3
   D Sentence 5

3. The word *not* should follow the helping verb in Sentence 6. Where should it go?
   A after *She*
   B after *will*
   C after *forget*
   D after *it*

4. In which sentence should the helping verb *is* go before the main verb?
   A Sentence 2
   B Sentence 4
   C Sentence 5
   D Sentence 6

5. Which does NOT have a helping verb?
   A Sentence 1
   B Sentence 4
   C Sentence 5
   D Sentence 6

6. Which are the main and helping verbs in Sentence 4?
   A *will* and *soon*
   B *will* and *become*
   C *soon* and *become*
   D *become* and *dark*

Grammar Practice Book
© Harcourt • Grade 3

▶ **Rewrite the sentences. Add a helping verb to each one.**

1. I never studied mammals.

   _____

2. We learn about bats.

   _____

3. We go to the library.

   _____

4. Butterflies see red, yellow, and green.

   _____

5. A butterfly landed on that leaf.

   _____

6. That butterfly laid 400 eggs.

   _____

7. Butterflies fly only when they are warm.

   _____

8. The librarian found a great book about butterflies.

   _____

Grammar Practice Book
© Harcourt • Grade 3

▶ **Rewrite each sentence. Use the correct present-tense form of the verb in parentheses ( ).**

1. I (help) my family.

_____

2. My sister (plant) carrot seeds.

_____

3. We (work) together in the garden.

_____

4. My brother (pick) tomatoes.

_____

5. My mother (carry) them inside.

_____

6. My father (wash) the tomatoes.

_____

7. He (slice) them into small pieces.

_____

8. I (make) a salad for dinner.

_____

9. A friend (eat) with us.

_____

10. She (enjoy) the salad.

_____

▶ **Write the verb in each sentence. Then write _S_ if the subject is singular or _P_ if the subject is plural.**

1. We plan a picnic. _____

2. I make sandwiches. _____

3. A dish breaks. _____

4. Lila fixes it with glue. _____

5. The children eat under a tree. _____

6. Teresa hears thunder. _____

7. They put the food away. _____

8. She runs home. _____

▶ **Rewrite each sentence. Use the correct present-tense form of the verb in parentheses ( ).**

9. Leah (like) this book.

_____

10. The prince (marry) the princess.

_____

11. He (write) a fairy tale.

_____

12. We (enjoy) the story.

_____

Name _____

▶ **Read this part of a student's rough draft. Then
answer the questions that follow.**

(1) My father and I make a cake for my brother's birthday.
(2) I mix the ingredients. (3) My father bake the cake in the
oven. (4) We ices it together. (5) My brother _____ the cake
at his party. (6) _____ loves it.

1. Which sentence has a
   singular subject and a correct
   present-tense verb?
   A Sentence 1
   B Sentence 2
   C Sentence 3
   D Sentence 4

2. Which sentence has a singular
   subject and an incorrect
   present-tense verb?
   A Sentence 1
   B Sentence 2
   C Sentence 3
   D Sentence 4

3. Which sentence has a
   plural subject and a correct
   present-tense verb?
   A Sentence 1
   B Sentence 2
   C Sentence 3
   D Sentence 4

4. Which sentence has a plural
   subject and an incorrect
   present-tense verb?
   A Sentence 1
   B Sentence 2
   C Sentence 3
   D Sentence 4

5. Which is a present-tense verb
   that could fill in the blank in
   Sentence 5?
   A eating
   B eat
   C eats
   D ate

6. Which subject could fill in the
   blank in Sentence 6?
   A He
   B We
   C He and his friends
   D My brother's friends

▶ **Rewrite each sentence correctly, using the subject in parentheses ( ). Be sure that the verb in your sentence agrees with its new subject.**

Example: Glenda likes math. (My brothers)

My brothers like math.

1. I enter a writing contest. (George)

   _____

2. The teachers judge the contest. (A teacher)

   _____

3. One student wins the contest. (Two students)

   _____

4. We like stories about animals. (You)

   _____

5. She prefers true stories. (He)

   _____

6. The princesses meet a prince. (The princess)

   _____

7. We hurry home from school. (They)

   _____

8. Our mother opens the front door. (We)

   _____

▶ **Write the verb in each sentence. Then label it as *present*, *past*, or *future* tense.**

1. Jen finishes her homework quickly.

   _____

2. Simon will write an essay next week.

   _____

3. The teacher assigned five math problems.

   _____

4. You carried a dictionary to school.

   _____

5. Students will read their reports aloud.

   _____

6. Jason draws a picture in art class.

   _____

7. We tried the science experiment at home.

   _____

8. The children named three kinds of plants.

   _____

9. My sister learns Spanish in high school.

   _____

10. I will ask my mother for help.

   _____

▶ **Rewrite each sentence. Use the future-tense form of the verb in parentheses ( ).**

1. Yolanda (stay) home from school today.

   _____

2. She (go) to the doctor later.

   _____

3. The doctor (give) her some medicine.

   _____

4. She (feel) much better tomorrow.

   _____

▶ **Write a sentence that uses the future-tense form of the verb.**

5. run

   _____

6. play

   _____

7. hurry

   _____

8. watch

   _____

▶ **Read this part of a student's rough draft. Then answer the questions that follow.**

(1) Paul _____ all week for today's math test. (2) Soon he take the test. (3) He clears his desk. (4) His teacher hands him the test sheet. (5) She smiles and says "Good luck." (6) Paul worked hard, and he will do well on the test.

1. Which verb form BEST completes Sentence 1?
   - A study
   - B will study
   - C studied
   - D studies

2. Which verb needs the helping verb *will* to make it a correct future-tense verb?
   - A take (Sentence 2)
   - B clears (Sentence 3)
   - C smiles (Sentence 5)
   - D worked (Sentence 6)

3. Which sentence does NOT have a present-tense verb?
   - A Sentence 3
   - B Sentence 4
   - C Sentence 5
   - D Sentence 6

4. Which sentence has two correct present-tense verbs?
   - A Sentence 3
   - B Sentence 4
   - C Sentence 5
   - D Sentence 6

5. Which sentence has a correct past-tense verb?
   - A Sentence 2
   - B Sentence 3
   - C Sentence 5
   - D Sentence 6

6. Which sentence has a correct future-tense verb?
   - A Sentence 3
   - B Sentence 4
   - C Sentence 5
   - D Sentence 6

▶ **Underline the verb in each sentence. Then rewrite the sentence in the tense shown in parentheses ( ).**

1. The children study quietly. (past)

   _____

2. The teacher will talk about the report. (past)

   _____

3. Many students enjoyed music class. (present)

   _____

4. Mr. Green scores the test. (future)

   _____

5. Tim will hurry to school. (present)

   _____

6. We play outside during recess. (past)

   _____

7. You solved the math problem. (future)

   _____

8. Misha practices the flute. (past)

   _____

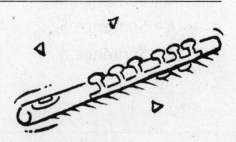

Grammar Practice Book
© Harcourt • Grade 3

▶ **Read this part of a student's rough draft. Then answer the questions that follow.**

> **(1)** Mia and Simon writing a story. **(2)** The story are about a robot. **(3)** The robot is funny. **(4)** It _____ say all sorts of things. **(5)** The children are excited. **(6)** They will show the story to their teacher.

1. Which sentence has a singular subject and the correct form of the verb *be*?
A Sentence 2
B Sentence 3
C Sentence 5
D Sentence 6

2. Which sentence has a plural subject and the correct form of the verb *be*?
A Sentence 2
B Sentence 3
C Sentence 5
D Sentence 6

3. Which sentence has a form of the verb *be* that does NOT agree with the subject?
A Sentence 2
B Sentence 3
C Sentence 5
D Sentence 6

4. Which helping verb should go before the main verb in Sentence 1?
A have
B will
C can
D are

5. Which helping verb could complete Sentence 4?
A have
B had
C can
D is

6. Which other helping verb could replace *will* in Sentence 6?
A had
B can
C have
D were

▶ **Read this part of a student's rough draft. Then answer the questions that follow.**

> (1) William loves space. (2) He looked at pictures of the sun and moon when he was younger. (3) Now he read books about the solar system. (4) He will learn about the planets. (5) He will studies space travel. (6) One day he will become an astronaut.

1. Which sentence has a correct past-tense verb?
   - A Sentence 1
   - B Sentence 2
   - C Sentence 4
   - D Sentence 5

2. Which sentence has a correct present-tense verb?
   - A Sentence 1
   - B Sentence 2
   - C Sentence 3
   - D Sentence 4

3. Which sentence has an incorrect form of a future-tense verb?
   - A Sentence 2
   - B Sentence 4
   - C Sentence 5
   - D Sentence 6

4. Which verb should end with an *s*?
   - A *looked* (Sentence 2)
   - B *read* (Sentence 3)
   - C *learn* (Sentence 4)
   - D *become* (Sentence 6)

5. Which is the future-tense form of the verb in Sentence 1?
   - A love
   - B will love
   - C will loves
   - D loved

6. Which is the past-tense form of the verb in Sentence 4?
   - A learn
   - B learns
   - C can learn
   - D learned

Name _____

▶ **Rewrite each sentence. Use the verb and tense shown in parentheses ( ).**

1. I _____ a spider yesterday. (*see*—past tense)

   _____

2. The spider _____ home to its web. (*go*—past tense)

   _____

3. Shondra _____ a pet spider. (*have*—past tense)

   _____

4. Zack _____ that he likes spiders. (*say*—present tense)

   _____

5. A spider _____ several things to catch insects. (*do*—present tense)

   _____

6. A fly _____ to the spider's web. (*come*—present tense)

   _____

7. That spider _____ (*have*—present tense) a sticky web.

   _____

8. The spider _____ (*do*—past tense) its work quickly.

   _____

▶ **Rewrite each sentence, using the correct present-tense verb in parentheses ( ).**

1. The tired pig (lies, lays) in the grass.

   _____

2. The sun (rises, raises) over the field.

   _____

3. The farmer (sits, sets) her bucket on a stool.

   _____

4. He (lies, lays) a blanket over the horse.

   _____

5. We (sit, set) together under an apple tree.

   _____

▶ **Rewrite each sentence. Use the past-tense form of the verb shown in parentheses ( ).**

6. Gwen _____ in the sun all afternoon. (lie)

   _____

7. The children _____ early for school. (rise)

   _____

8. You _____ the eggs on the table. (set)

   _____

9. The hen _____ many eggs. (lay)

   _____

▶ **Read this part of a student's rough draft. Then
answer the questions that follow.**

(1) The sun risen, and it was a beautiful morning. (2) Nathan
_____ in the grass. (3) He watched as three deer came to the river.
(4) Nathan saw the deer drink. (5) He say nothing, because he did not
want to scare them. (6) When the deer had finished drinking, Nathan
_____ to his feet and walked quietly home.

1. Which verb form could go in
   the blank in Sentence 2?
   A lays
   B laid
   C lain
   D lay

2. Which is the present-tense
   form of the verb *saw* in
   Sentence 4?
   A did seen
   B had seen
   C had see
   D sees

3. Which is a correct past-tense
   verb to replace the underlined
   verb in Sentence 5?
   A says
   B sayed
   C said
   D saying

4. Which verb needs the helping
   verb *had* before it?
   A risen (Sentence 1)
   B saw (Sentence 4)
   C drink (Sentence 4)
   D scare (Sentence 5)

5. Which are the present-tense
   forms of the verbs in
   Sentence 3?
   A watches, come
   B did watch, had come
   C had watched, had come
   D will watch, will come

6. Which verb form could go in
   the blank in Sentence 6?
   A rise
   B rose
   C raise
   D raised

Name _____

► **Rewrite each sentence, using the verb tense in parentheses ( ).**

1. The spider laid eggs. (present tense)

   _____

2. I have two books on spiders. (past tense)

   _____

3. The farmer's daughter had done her chores. (present tense)

   _____

4. She sits at the kitchen table. (past tense)

   _____

5. Her brother comes home from school. (past tense)

   _____

6. He will say "giddyup" to the horse. (past tense)

   _____

7. The neighbors raised their new flag. (present tense)

   _____

8. We saw many animals on the farm. (present tense)

   _____

Grammar Practice Book
© Harcourt • Grade 3

► **Write the adverb in each sentence. Then write whether it tells *how*, *where*, or *when*.**

1. Ants work together in colonies. _____

2. We saw an ant hill outside. _____

3. I observed ants earlier. _____

4. You touched one ant gently. _____

5. Soon the ants will dig a nest. _____

6. Some ants left a trail here. _____

7. The big ant moves slowly. _____

8. Wow, those ants go everywhere! _____

9. The ants carefully carry a bread crumb. _____

10. Worker ants always care for their queen. _____

11. Now the ants walk in a line. _____

12. Those ants live underground. _____

Try This

Write three sentences about your day at school. Use an adverb in each sentence. One adverb should tell *how*, one should tell *where*, and one should tell *when*.

▶ **Rewrite each sentence. Use the correct comparative form of the adverb in parentheses ( ).**

1. This ant works (hard) than that ant.

   _____

2. Which butterfly flies the (low)?

   _____

3. The shark swims (fast) than the fish.

   _____

4. That dolphin jumps the (high) of all.

   _____

5. These birds will fly south (soon) than those birds.

   _____

▶ **Rewrite each sentence. Add _more_ or _the most_ before the adverb.**

6. The nightingale sings _____ beautifully of all the birds.

   _____

7. A tiger moves _____ quietly than an elephant.

   _____

8. The horse drinks _____ often than the camel.

   _____

9. My dog wags its tail _____ happily of all.

   _____

▶ **Read this part of a student's rough draft. Then answer the questions that follow.**

(1) I like science, and I work hard. (2) Yesterday I read about spiders. (3) Today I studied the planets. (4) I learned that Earth spins _____ than Mercury. (5) I also learned that Mercury moves around the sun the _____ of all the planets. (6) I will visit a science museum soon, and I will learn more there.

1. Which word does the adverb in Sentence 1 describe?

A I

B like

C science

D work

2. Which sentence has an adverb that tells *how*?

A Sentence 1

B Sentence 2

C Sentence 3

D Sentence 6

3. Which sentence has an adverb that tells *where*?

A Sentence 1

B Sentence 2

C Sentence 3

D Sentence 6

4. Which sentence does NOT have an adverb that tells *when*?

A Sentence 1

B Sentence 2

C Sentence 3

D Sentence 6

5. Which form of an adverb could go in the blank in Sentence 4?

A fast

B faster

C more faster

D fastest

6. Which form of an adverb could go in the blank in Sentence 5?

A quick

B quickly

C most quickly

D more quickly

Name _____

▶ **Write the adverb in each sentence. Then write the verb that it describes.**

1. My teacher talks excitedly about science.

   _____

2. Tomorrow we will learn about insects.

   _____

3. Of all the students, Evan studied the longest.

   _____

4. I speak more softly than the other students at the library.

   _____

▶ **Rewrite each sentence. Complete it with an adverb that answers the question in parentheses ( ).**

5. This spider crawls _____ than that spider. (How?)

   _____

6. I put my report _____. (Where?)

   _____

7. _____ you will learn about the sun. (When?)

   _____

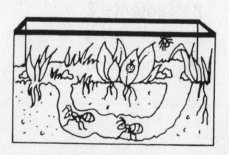

98

► **Rewrite each sentence. Replace the underlined words with a contraction.**

1. <u>It is</u> an exciting day.

   _____

2. <u>I am</u> going to be in a baking contest.

   _____

3. Some children <u>did not</u> know about the contest.

   _____

4. <u>You are</u> bringing two pies.

   _____

5. My brothers <u>are not</u> baking anything.

   _____

6. They <u>had not</u> entered the contest.

   _____

7. The judges <u>were not</u> in the room.

   _____

8. <u>They are</u> eager to taste my cookies.

   _____

9. My father <u>could not</u> come to the contest.

   _____

10. We <u>should not</u> eat too much cake.

    _____

Name _____

► **Rewrite each sentence, using the correct word(s) in parentheses ( ).**

1. You hadn't (ever, never) told me about volcanoes.

   _____

2. I don't know (nothing, anything) about them.

   _____

3. My brother hasn't won (any, no) science prizes yet.

   _____

4. My sister doesn't have (none, any) either.

   _____

5. We haven't told (anybody, nobody) about the contest.

   _____

6. Laurie wouldn't tell her friends (neither, either).

   _____

7. Carlos won't go (anywhere, nowhere) without a notebook.

   _____

8. Isn't (no one, anyone) in the classroom?

   _____

9. Those children never enter (any, no) contests.

   _____

10. No one said (nothing, anything) about cleaning up.

    _____

▶ **Read this part of a student's rough draft. Then answer the questions that follow.**

(1) Maria is not going to give up! (2) She is making an electric buzzer for her science project. (3) She has not ever made one before, but her teacher showed her how. (4) Now Maria doesn't even need no help. (5) Maria's teacher smiles at her. (6) _____ glad that she's in his class.

1. Which sentence has a contraction that is formed with a pronoun?
- A Sentence 2
- B Sentence 4
- C Sentence 5
- D Sentence 6

2. Which sentence has a contraction that is formed with the word *not*?
- A Sentence 1
- B Sentence 4
- C Sentence 5
- D Sentence 6

3. Which sentence does NOT have two words that could form a contraction?
- A Sentence 1
- B Sentence 2
- C Sentence 3
- D Sentence 5

4. In which sentence could you form a contraction that includes a subject pronoun?
- A Sentence 1
- B Sentence 2
- C Sentence 4
- D Sentence 5

5. Which is a correct contraction that could go in the blank in Sentence 6?
- A He's
- B Hes'
- C He'd
- D He're

6. Which sentence has an error in it?
- A Sentence 2
- B Sentence 3
- C Sentence 4
- D Sentence 5

Name _____

▶ **Rewrite each sentence. Replace each contraction with the words used to form it.**

1. Alice doesn't see that we're waving.

   _____

2. She's worried that we haven't arrived.

   _____

3. I'm glad that you didn't stay home.

   _____

4. It isn't clear that he's the winner.

   _____

▶ **If the sentence is correct, write *correct*. If it is not, rewrite it correctly.**

5. Wouldn't you like any help?

   _____

6. I don't see my teacher nowhere.

   _____

7. There wasn't nobody in the cafeteria.

   _____

102

Name _____

▶ **Rewrite each sentence. Use capital letters and commas correctly.**

1. my father my sister and i watch the stars every night.

   _____

2. we sit outside in june july and august.

   _____

3. there is a telescope at school and i can use it.

   _____

4. mrs. morgan helps us point the telescope toward mars.

   _____

5. on monday we look at jupiter but on tuesday we look at saturn.

   _____

6. the sky is bright with fireworks on independence day.

   _____

7. i lie in the grass close my eyes and listen.

   _____

8. karen learns about the planets at lincoln elementary school.

   _____

9. she reads books looks at pictures and asks questions.

   _____

10. students can watch a short movie or they can read quietly.

   _____

► **Rewrite each title correctly. The words in parentheses ( ) tell what kind of title each one is.**

1. Charlie and the Chocolate Factory (book)

   _____

2. In Which Piglet Is Entirely Surrounded by Water (chapter from a book)

   _____

3. Hickory, Dickory, Dock (song)

   _____

4. Ranger Rick (magazine)

   _____

5. Lake Country Gazette (newspaper)

   _____

► **Rewrite each sentence. Write titles correctly.**

6. Have you read the book Little House on the Prairie?

   _____

7. My little sister likes the song Three Blind Mice.

   _____

8. Robert Louis Stevenson wrote a poem called The Lamplighter.

   _____

9. Students Speak is a column in our school newspaper.

   _____

Name _____

▶ **Read this part of a student's rough draft. Then answer the questions that follow.**

> (1) Mr. mercado is my neighbor and he knows a lot about the stars. (2) he gave me a book called find the constellations. (3) My brother my best friend and i read the book together. (4) We learned that there is a group of stars named Ursa Major. (5) they are supposed to look like a bear but they just look like pretty stars to me.

1. Which sentence is NOT missing one or more commas?
   A Sentence 1
   B Sentence 2
   C Sentence 3
   D Sentence 5

2. Which sentence needs two commas?
   A Sentence 1
   B Sentence 2
   C Sentence 3
   D Sentence 5

3. Which sentence has a proper noun that should be capitalized?
   A Sentence 1
   B Sentence 3
   C Sentence 4
   D Sentence 5

4. Which sentence does NOT have a pronoun that should be capitalized?
   A Sentence 1
   B Sentence 2
   C Sentence 3
   D Sentence 5

5. Which sentence has a title that should be capitalized and underlined?
   A Sentence 1
   B Sentence 2
   C Sentence 3
   D Sentence 4

6. Which sentence has a correct proper noun?
   A Sentence 1
   B Sentence 2
   C Sentence 3
   D Sentence 4

▶ **Rewrite each sentence correctly.**

1. sometimes i sing my favorite song.

   _____

2. that song is called twinkle, twinkle, little star.

   _____

3. those three stars are named altair castor and polaris.

   _____

4. sirius is the brightest star in the sky and i see it at night.

   _____

5. you can read about stars in a magazine called Ask.

   _____

6. mrs. wong reads to children at the library in middletown.

   _____

7. she lives in new york but she works in connecticut.

   _____

8. today she reads the book a child's introduction to the night sky.

   _____

Grammar Practice Book

© Harcourt • Grade 3

▶ **Read this part of a student's rough draft. Then answer the questions that follow.**

> (1) Yesterday my class went to an animal park. (2) We saw lions from the window of the school bus. (3) One lion _____ on a rock. (4) Monkeys played happily in the trees. (5) Some of them come excitedly to the bus. (6) _____, I will write a story about all the animals I seen.

1. Which of these verb forms could go in the blank in Sentence 3?
A sit
B sets
C sat
D set

2. Which verb needs the helping verb *have* before it?
A went (Sentence 1)
B saw (Sentence 2)
C write (Sentence 6)
D seen (Sentence 6)

3. Which is the past-tense form that could replace the underlined verb in Sentence 5?
A comes
B comed
C came
D camed

4. Which sentence has an adverb that tells *when*?
A Sentence 1
B Sentence 2
C Sentence 4
D Sentence 5

5. Which sentence does NOT have an adverb?
A Sentence 1
B Sentence 2
C Sentence 4
D Sentence 5

6. Which adverb could go in the blank in Sentence 6?
A Tomorrow
B More quickly
C Most slowly
D More slow

▶ **Read this part of a student's rough draft. Then answer the questions that follow.**

(1) Latisha, Latisha's father and his friend went to Tonto National Forest in Arizona. (2) They _____ stay long but they had a great time. (3) They camped, hiked and swam on friday. (4) On Saturday night they sang a song around the campfire called "Make New Friends." (5) Latisha didn't never want to leave the forest.

1. Which sentence has a contraction?
   A Sentence 1
   B Sentence 3
   C Sentence 4
   D Sentence 5

2. Which contraction could go in the blank in Sentence 2?
   A doesn't
   B aren't
   C couldn't
   D they're

3. Which sentence has a double negative that needs to be corrected?
   A Sentence 1
   B Sentence 3
   C Sentence 4
   D Sentence 5

4. Which of these sentences does NOT need a comma added?
   A Sentence 1
   B Sentence 2
   C Sentence 3
   D Sentence 5

5. Which of these sentences has a proper noun that is incorrect?
   A Sentence 1
   B Sentence 3
   C Sentence 4
   D Sentence 5

6. Which sentence is correct?
   A Sentence 1
   B Sentence 3
   C Sentence 4
   D Sentence 5

INDEX

N

Negatives, 99–102, 108

Nouns

capitalization of, 24–26, 35

common, 23, 25–26

possessive, 37–40, 53

proper, 23–26, 35

singular and plural, 31–34, 36

See also Abbreviations; Titles

O

Object pronouns, 45–48, 53–54

P

Past-tense verbs, 85, 87–88, 90–94, 107

Plural nouns, 31–34, 36

Plural possessive nouns, 37–40

Plural pronouns, 42–44

Possessive nouns, 37–40, 53

Predicates

complete, 9–12, 18

compound, 13–16, 18

simple, 10–12

Present-tense verbs, 81–85, 87–88, 90–94, 107

Pronouns

antecedents of, 49–54

singular and plural, 41–44

subject and object, 45–48, 53–54

Proper nouns, 23–26, 35

Punctuation, 103–106

apostrophes in contractions, 99–102, 108

Punctuation (con't)

apostrophes in possessive nouns, 38

commas, 14–16, 20–21, 103, 105

end marks, 1–8, 17

Q

Questions, 2–4

S

Sentences

capitalization of, 1–6, 17, 103, 105

compound, 19–22, 35

simple, 19, 35

Sentences, kinds of

declarative, 1–4

exclamatory, 5–8

imperative, 5–8

interrogative, 2–4

Simple predicates, 10–12

Simple sentences, 19, 35

Simple subjects, 9, 11–12, 18

Singular nouns, 31–34, 36

Singular possessive nouns, 37–40

Singular pronouns, 41, 43–44

Statements, 1–4

Subject pronouns, 45–48, 53–54

Subject-verb agreement, 68–70, 73–76, 81–84, 89–90

Subjects

complete, 11–12

compound, 13–16, 18

simple, 9, 11–12, 18

Grammar Practice Book

© Harcourt • Grade 3